The Baby Uggs Are Hatching

by **Jack Prelutsky**
pictures by
James Stevenson

Greenwillow Books, New York

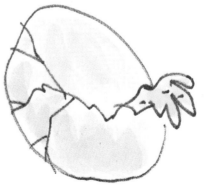

Library of Congress
Cataloging in Publication Data
Prelutsky, Jack.
The baby uggs are hatching.
Summary: A collection of twelve humorous
poems about such strange creatures as
the sneepy and the quossible.
1. Children's poetry, American.
2. Humorous poetry, American.
[1. American poetry. 2 Humorous poetry]
I. Stevenson, James (date), ill.
II Title.
PS3566.R36B3   811'.54   81-7266
ISBN 0-688-00922-0   AACR2
ISBN 0-688-00923-9 (lib. bdg.)

TO WILLIAM COLE
FOR THIS AND THAT

Contents

The Baby Uggs Are Hatching

The baby Uggs are hatching
   out of their ugly eggs,
here come their ugly bodies,
here come their ugly legs,
out of their shells they scramble,
fierce and fat and fleet,
back and forth they shamble
on their little ugly feet.

uggily wuggily zuggily zee
the baby Uggs are fierce and free,
uggily wuggily zuggily zay
the baby Uggs come out today.

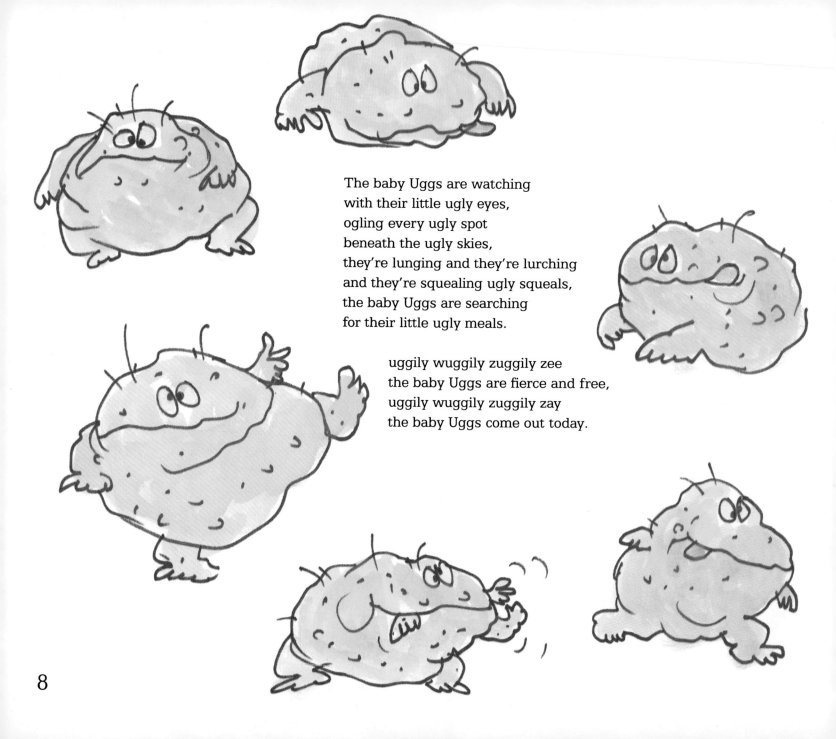

The baby Uggs are watching
with their little ugly eyes,
ogling every ugly spot
beneath the ugly skies,
they're lunging and they're lurching
and they're squealing ugly squeals,
the baby Uggs are searching
for their little ugly meals.

uggily wuggily zuggily zee
the baby Uggs are fierce and free,
uggily wuggily zuggily zay
the baby Uggs come out today.

The baby Uggs are snatching
as they creep along the beach,
gobbling every ugly thing
within their ugly reach,
some gobble down each other
as across the crags they crawl,
and the Uggs that eat their mothers
are the ugliest Uggs of all.

uggily wuggily zuggily zee
the baby Uggs are fierce and free,
uggily wuggily zuggily zay
the baby Uggs come out today. □

9

The Quossible

The Quossible, the Quossible,
its habits are impossible,
its temper is irascible,
its manners are not passable.

A critter very crittery,
its fangs are glinty, glittery,
its limbs are slick and slithery,
its face is weird and withery.

The Quossible's deplorable,
its size is unignorable,
its body's big and blundery,
its voice is thick and thundery.

Its appetite is sizable,
its methods are despisable,
it moves about all creepily

. . . its diet is all people-y. □

The Sneepies

T he Sneepies, lying in a heap,
are almost always fast asleep.
Deep inside my dresser drawer
they sleep and sleep, but do not snore.

The Sneepies, lying in a pile,
are still and silent all the while.
They stay beside my underwear . . .
I wonder why they like it there. ☐

The Smasheroo

The Smasheroo, the Smasheroo!
It loved to smash things up,
it smashed a million mirrors
and at least as many cups,
it broke a batch of bottles
into bits as big as beans,
and shattered stacks of saucers
into scads of smithereens.

14

It devastated dishes,
it disintegrated clocks,
it demolished chairs and tables
and it decimated rocks,
but alas it grew too reckless
in its smashing sort of way,
and that is why the Smasheroo
is not around today.

One afternoon it stumbled
on a tiny baby Greep,
and pulverized its rattle
as the infant lay asleep,
but Mama Greep was watching,
in a fury up she flew,
and in half a dozen seconds
Mama smashed the Smasheroo. □

The Nimpy-Numpy-Numpity

The Nimpy-Numpy-Numpity
is big and bad and bumpity,
its head is huge and humpity,
its limbs are long and lumpity.

The Nimpy-Numpy-Numpity
is dirty, dumb and dumpity,
but most of all,
yes most of all,
oh absolutely most of all,

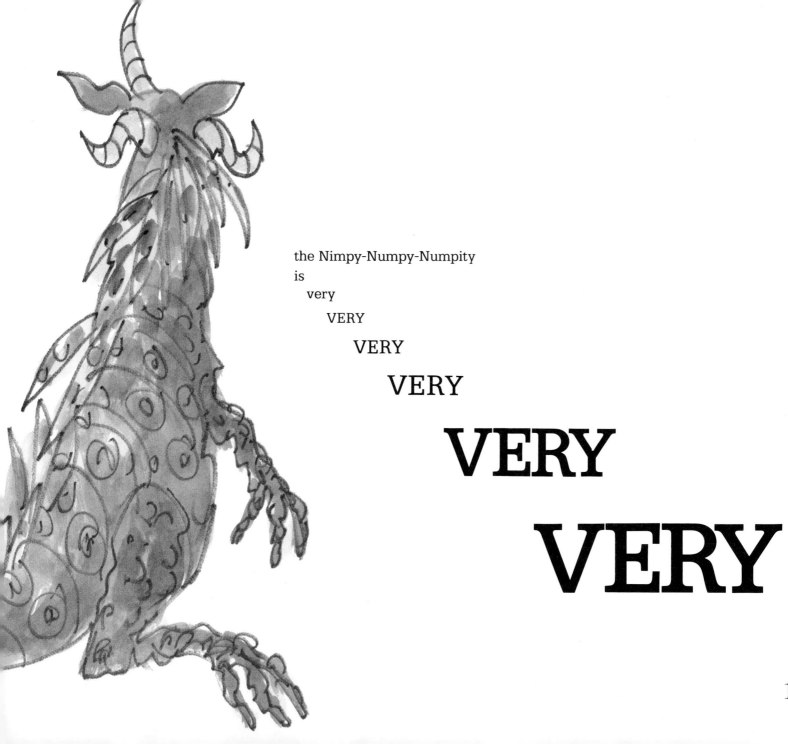

the Nimpy-Numpy-Numpity
is
   very
      VERY
         VERY
            VERY

VERY

VERY

17

GRUMPITY!

The Sneezysnoozer

T he Sneezysnoozer sneezes
as the Sneezysnoozer chooses,
it snoozes as it pleases
and it sneezes as it snoozes,
as it rises, as it pauses,
as it dozes, as it lazes,
and it sneezes with no causes
as it muses, as it grazes.

The Sneezysnoozer sneezes
in a dozen sneezy sizes,
it sneezes little breezes
and it sneezes big surprises
and it sneezes teeny wheezes,
so it easily amuses
when the Sneezysnoozer sneezes
as the Sneezysnoozer chooses. ☐

21

The Snatchits

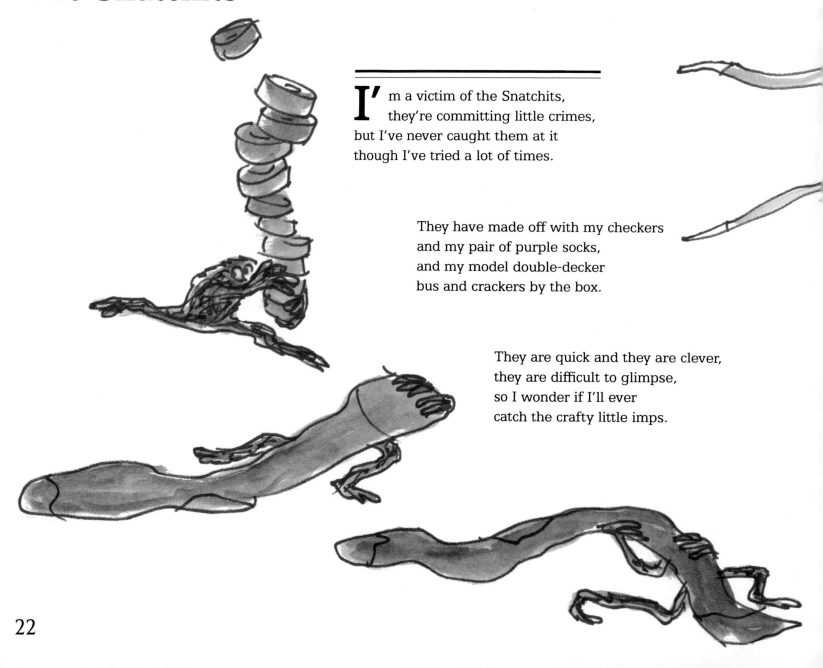

I'm a victim of the Snatchits,
    they're committing little crimes,
but I've never caught them at it
though I've tried a lot of times.

They have made off with my checkers
and my pair of purple socks,
and my model double-decker
bus and crackers by the box.

They are quick and they are clever,
they are difficult to glimpse,
so I wonder if I'll ever
catch the crafty little imps.

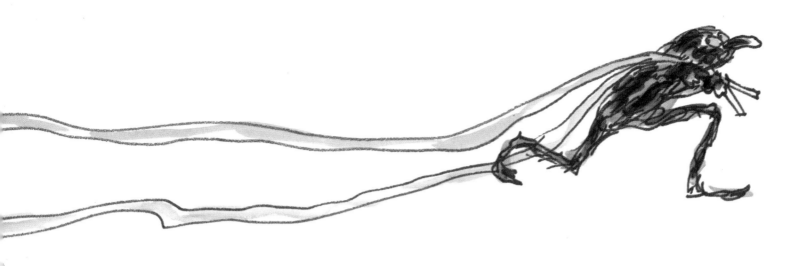

Just today the tiny fellows
swiped the laces from my shoes
and a crayon (it was yellow)
as I took a little snooze.

And they carried off my hatchet
and some buttons from my clothes,
if I ever catch a Snatchit
I will bop that Snatchit's nose. ☐

The Dreary Dreeze

Oh do not fear the dreary Dreeze,
it surely means no harm,
it may seem somewhat sleazy
but there's no need for alarm,
for it only wants to squeeze you
with its dreezy little arm.

And should it squeeze you harder
than you care to have a squeeze,
why then you only have to say,
"Dear Dreeze! I do not care to play,
so do not squeeze me, dreary Dreeze,
I do not like the way you squeeze."
And it will answer, "As you please!"
. . . and softly ease away. ☐

The Slithery Slitch

The slithery Slitch, the slimy Slitch,
the richest of the monster rich
lives within a silver ditch
in fancy Monstertown.
He haunts the finest monster shops
and buys the finest monster slops
and slick and slimy monster drops—
then pops the slime all down.

A maid sweeps up his slimy stones
and stacks the slimy skulls he owns,
a chef prepares him slimy bones
and pounds of slimy meat.
He swallows mounds of slimy bread,
then slips into his slimy bed
where butlers oil his slimy head
and grease his slimy feet.

Inside his slimy limousine
that slips about the slimy scene
he guzzles a glass of gasoline
and licks his slimy lips.
With rings on either slimy hand
he's a monster glorious, great and grand,
the wealthiest in monster land,
the slithery slimy Slitch. ☐

The Creature in the Classroom

It appeared inside our classroom
at a quarter after ten,
it gobbled up the blackboard,
three erasers and a pen.
It gobbled teacher's apple
and it bopped her with the core.
"How dare you!" she responded.
"You must leave us . . . there's the door."

The creature didn't listen
but described an arabesque
as it gobbled all her pencils,
seven notebooks and her desk.
Teacher stated very calmly,
"Sir! you simply cannot stay.
I'll report you to the principal
unless you go away!"

But the thing continued eating,
it ate paper, swallowed ink.
As it gobbled up our homework,
I believe I saw it wink.
Teacher finally lost her temper.
"OUT!" she shouted at the creature.
The creature hopped beside her
and GLOPP . . . it gobbled teacher. ☐

29

Grubby Grebbles

There's a group of grubby Grebbles
that is slowly going by,
it's unlikely that you'll see them
so you might as well not try,
for that group of grubby Grebbles
only travel underground,
so you never can be certain
when the Grebbles are around.

They chew gravel as they travel,
they eat sandwiches of slate,
grubby Grebbles munch on marble
as they slowly excavate,
Grebbles tunnel through the planet
gnawing granite by the ton,
rocks are breakfast, lunch and supper
for the Grebble garrison.

All they ever drink is lava,
all they ever eat is stone,
it may ail their Grebble bellies
but the Grebbles never groan;
all that lies inside a mountain
is a feast for grubby Grebbles,
larger Grebbles gobble boulders,
little Grebbles nibble pebbles. □

30

The Flotterzott

When days are hot,
the Flotterzott
slides right outside its skin,

and when it's not,
the Flotterzott
goes sliding right back in. ☐

32